CAFFEINATED
IDEAS
Journal

yellow pear  press

Text copyright © 2015 by Lisa McGuinness.

Illustrations copyright © 2015 by Danielle Kroll.

ISBN: 978-0-9905370-0-7

Library of Congress Cataloging-in-Publication data available upon request.

Manufactured in Hong Kong.

Design by Danielle Kroll.

This book has been set in Bembo.

10 9 8 7 6 5 4 3 2 1

Yellow Pear Press, LLC.
www.yellowpearpress.com

Distributed by Publishers Group West

To Matt,

who's nice to me even before he's had his morning coffee.

TABLE OF CONTENTS

Introduction

Does caffeine truly make us more creative and inspired or just wake us up enough to actually think? Many incredibly creative people throughout history—from Honoré de Balzac to Gary Larson—have given kudos to the powers of the coffee bean and tea leaf and have noted that caffeine—in one form or another—has been an important part of their creative rituals.

With the right attitude, and a morning espresso, it is possible to be inspired. The goal is to create ideas wherever you are. So, go ahead and observe and reflect on the grand and small ways that you can change things up. Pay attention to your ideas and write them down so they become real instead of fleeting snippets. Incorporate the good ones into your life like friends and don't worry about the silly ones. No one will ever know.

Some thoughts will need to percolate until they can be achieved, while others will be easily accomplished. Don't box yourself in by worrying about failure or whether your ideas are subpar. The Irish poet Samuel Beckett wrote, "Ever tried. Ever failed. No matter. Try again. Fail again. Fail better."

So pay attention. Write your ideas on these pages. Tuck this little book in your purse or backpack. Put it on your bedside table or in the glove box of your car. Scrawl in it. Underline things that catch your attention. Doodle.

Anna Quindlen said, "You are the only person alive who has sole custody of your life." Keep that in mind when you write down your thoughts, ideas, and moments of inspiration. Make them real. Make them you. When you're ready to flesh them out, have a delicious caffeinated beverage and let the neurons start firing!

Espresso Ideas

"This coffee falls into your stomach, and straightway there is a general commotion. Ideas begin to move like the battalions of the Grand Army of the battlefield. Similes arise, the paper is covered with ink; for the struggle commences and is concluded with torrents of black water..." —Honoré de Balzac

Once, while working at a book fair in Bologna, Italy, a co-worker and I emerged from a cigarette smoke-filled conference center at the end of a long day. We were in serious need of caffeine. We stopped at coffee bar where a barista told my cohort to "Drink it very fast!" as he passed the espresso over the counter. He tossed it back like a shot of tequila and then sighed in ecstasy. Sometimes ideas sprint around the brain like the jolt of this sassy drink. If you have an idea about something that is as quick and satisfying as downing an espresso, jot it here.

Espresso

1½ OUNCES DARK ROAST COFFEE BEANS, *finely ground*

4 OUNCES WATER, *30 seconds off the boil*

SUGAR OR SWEETENER *(optional)*

Using an espresso maker, force boiled water through the finely

ground beans. Pour the espresso into a warmed espresso cup

and add sugar as desired.

Makes 1 serving.

Cappuccino Ideas

"Coffee induces wit. Take it without sugar—very swank: gives the impression you have lived in the East." —Gustave Flaubert

Sometimes ideas require not just a jolt, but something a little more complex. Espresso and foam don't mix much, nothing like a latte, but steamed milk adds flavor and texture. Cappuccino Ideas are less straightforward than Espresso Ideas. Sometimes they happen quickly—after all, a small cup does the job—but these inspirations may need to be tempered with consideration before rushing to make them real. There are several ways to make cappuccino, but this recipe is my favorite because it's not too milky.

Cappuccino

1 SHOT (1½ OUNCES) ESPRESSO *(see Espresso recipe, page 9)*

1½ OUNCES STEAMED MILK *(of your choice)*

1½ OUNCES MILK FOAM

SUGAR OR SWEETENER *(optional)*

GROUND COCOA POWDER, CINNAMON, NUTMEG AND/OR VANILLA POWDER *(optional)*

Pour the shot of espresso (or coffee) into a cappuccino cup. Steam the milk
until it's piping hot and foamy and then spoon milk and foam onto the espresso.
Add sugar as desired. Sprinkle ground cocoa powder, cinnamon, nutmeg or
vanilla powder on top if you'd like.

Makes 1 serving.

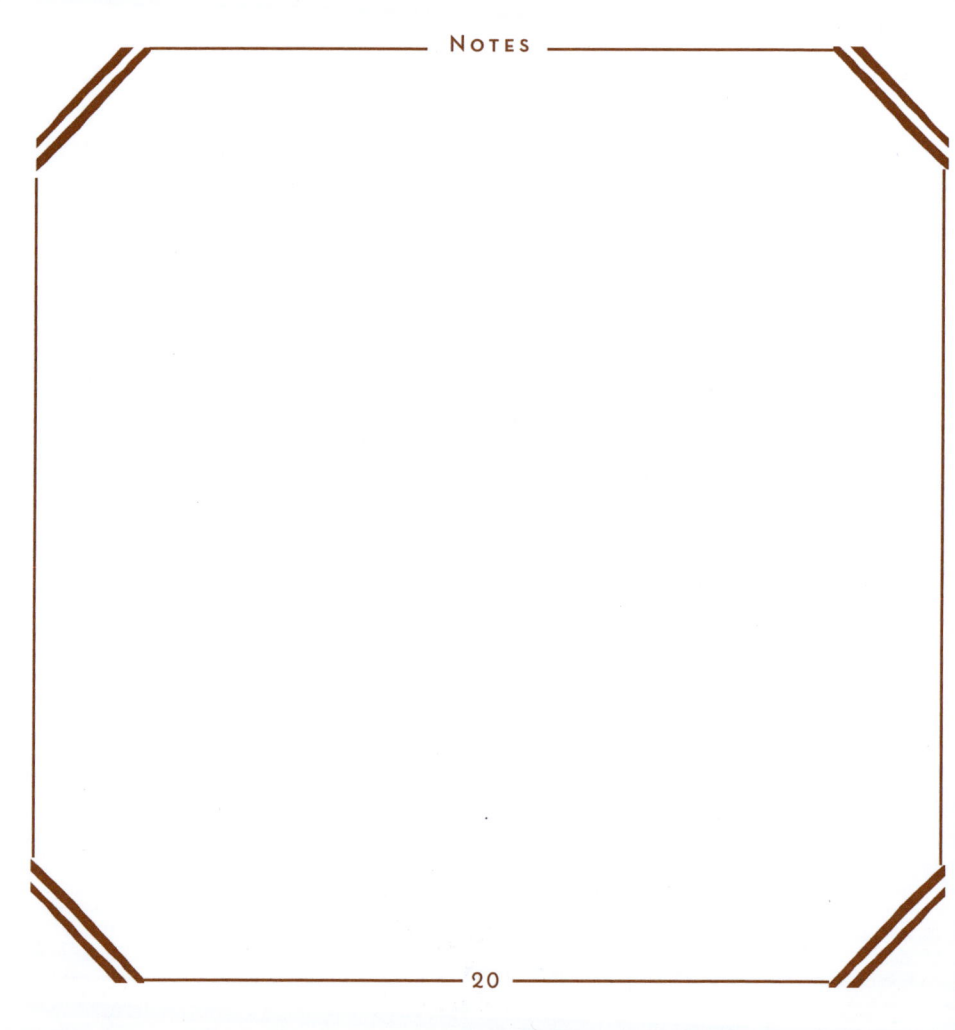

NOTES

Caffé Latte Ideas

"I don't know where my ideas come from. I will admit, however, that one key ingredient is caffeine. I get a couple cups of coffee into me and weird things just start to happen."

—Gary Larson

A substantial caffé latte—replete with a cup of milk—is practically a protein shake for the inspired mind's ideas. If you have an idea that's going to take some mental brawn to activate, this is your Caffé Latte Idea. Not only will you have caffeine coursing through your veins and tickling your creativity, but this milky concoction will feed your body as well.

Caffé Latte

1 CUP (8 OUNCES) MILK *(of your choice)*

1 DOLLOP MILK FOAM

1 SHOT (1½ OUNCES) ESPRESSO OR VERY STRONG COFFEE *(see Espresso recipe, page 9)*

SUGAR OR SWEETENER *(optional)*

Steam the milk until it's piping hot and a layer of milk foam forms on the top.

Pour the liquid part into a latte glass, latte bowl, or tall coffee mug. Add the

shot of espresso to the steamed milk and then top with a dollop of milk foam.

Add sugar as desired.

Makes 1 serving

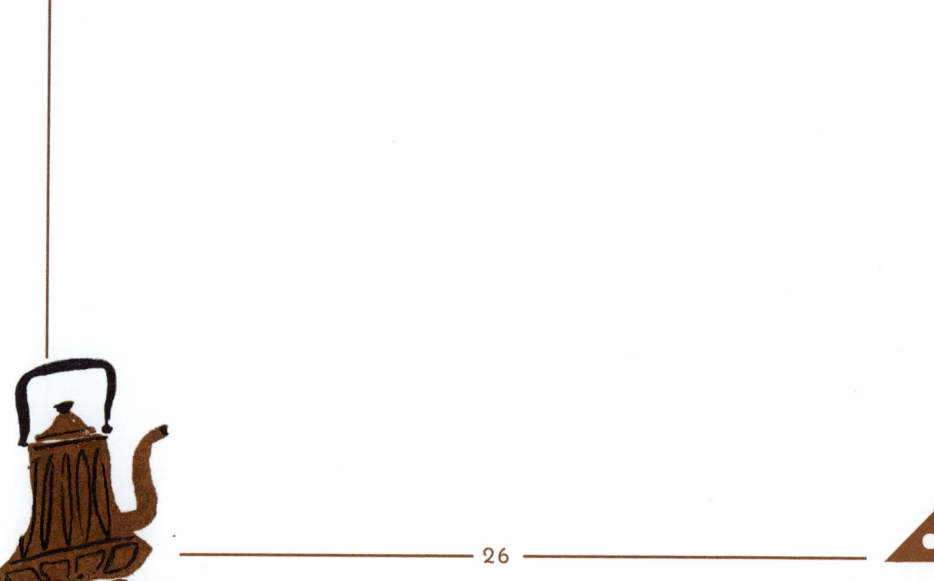

CAFFÉ AMERICANO IDEAS

"Voltaire had knocked back fifty cups of it a day. . . so he took it upon himself to make sure the coffee was good." —Phil Ford

As aspirational as the coffee's American namesake, Caffé Americano Ideas are like the American dream. This is the section where you can jot down your fantasy "to do" list. Who do you want to become? What do you want to do with your life? If you're feeling beaten down and afraid to even secretly admit the changes you want to make, remember this: falling down is part of life. Getting back up is living. So, write your Caffé Americano Ideas here, and no one will be the wiser. You might peek at where you wish to be someday and find yourself there. You'll look back at your notes and smile.

Caffé Americano

1 SHOT (1½ OUNCES) ESPRESSO *(see Espresso recipe, page 9)*

½ CUP (4 OUNCES) HOT WATER

SUGAR OR SWEETENER *(optional)*

Pour espresso into a cappuccino cup. Add hot water.

Stir in sugar as desired.

Makes 1 serving

CAFFÉ MOCHA IDEAS

"Fueled by my inspiration, I ran across the room to steal the cup of coffee the bookshelf had taken prisoner. Lapping the black watery brew like a hyena, I tossed the empty cup aside. I then returned to the chair to continue my divine act of creation. Hot blood swished in my head as my mighty pen stole across the page."

—Roman Payne from *Rooftop Soliloquy*

When you mix coffee and chocolate to create the sumptuous caffé mocha, you get a little bit of naughty and a little bit of nice. (You can decide which is which.) Your inspiration or idea that fits this bill (Naughty? Nice? A little of both?) is your Caffé Mocha Idea, and it belongs on the following pages.

Caffé Mocha

1 SHOT (1½ OUNCES) ESPRESSO *(see Espresso recipe, page 9)*

¾ CUP (6 OUNCES) MILK *(of your choice)*

2 TEASPOONS HOT CHOCOLATE POWDER OR CHOCOLATE SYRUP

SUGAR OR SWEETENER *(optional)*

WHIPPED CREAM *(optional)*

GROUND COCOA POWDER *(optional)*

Pour one shot of espresso into a coffee mug and set aside. Heat your favorite kind of milk in a saucepan (do not bring to a boil) and then remove from heat. Add hot chocolate powder to the hot milk and stir until well blended and smooth. Pour the chocolate milk into the coffee mug with the espresso and stir until evenly mixed. Add sugar to taste and top with whipped cream and ground cocoa powder if desired.

Makes 1 serving

French Press Coffee Ideas

"I have measured out my life in coffee spoons." —T.S. Eliot

Some ideas require the melding of time, patience, and inspiration to become gradually infused with rich-flavored meaning. Here's a place to note ideas that need steeping in order to become fully infused with understanding. Sometimes there's a snippet of an idea—a niggling of promise at the edge of your brain. You can feel the neurons firing, but the thought isn't quite formed. This is a French Press Coffee Idea. Write down what you can and let your mind gradually finish the idea. Occasionally revisit your notes, allowing your thoughts to eventually become complete, just like scalding hot water transforms into delicious coffee after swirling around with the rich, flavorful grounds in the French press.

French Press Coffee

3 TABLESPOONS COARSELY GROUND DARK-ROAST COFFEE BEANS

4 CUPS (32 OUNCES) WATER

MILK OF YOUR CHOICE *(optional)*

SUGAR OR SWEETENER *(optional)*

Place the coffee grounds at the bottom of a French press. Bring water to a boil and then pour over the coffee grounds. Place the top of the French press in place but do not press down the plunger. Allow the coffee to steep for 4 to 5 minutes. Press and pour into the cup of your choice. Add milk and sugar if desired.

Makes up to 3 servings depending on cup size

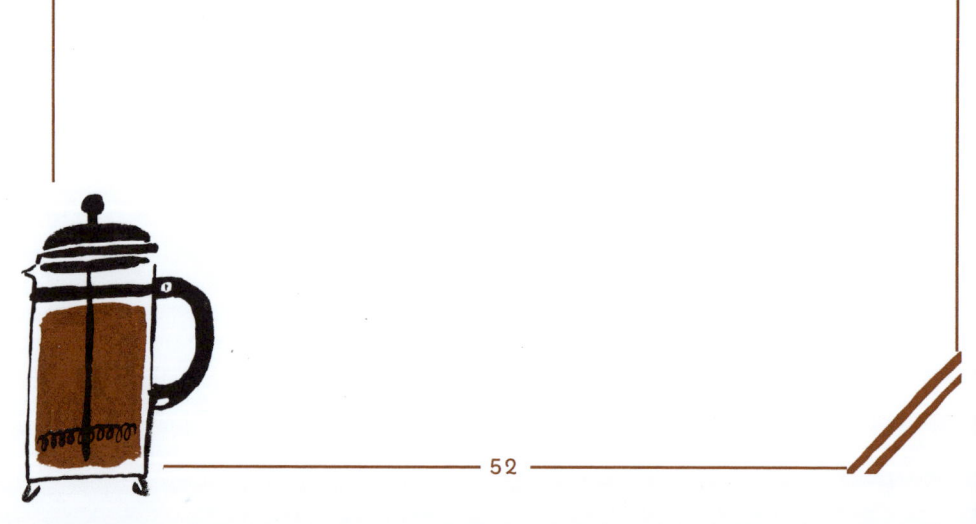

DRIP COFFEE IDEAS

"Without my morning coffee I'm just like a dried up piece of roast goat."
—Johann Sebastian Bach

What do you feel like you should know? What minutiae have you pondered, one drop at a time? There are some things—important or not—that a person just wants to understand. These musings are Drip Coffee Ideas. What do you want to learn? Does everyone else seem to know something that you don't? Here's the place to jot those questions down. Make a list and, over a nice, old-fashioned cup of joe, investigate the answers.

Drip Coffee

3 TABLESPOONS FINELY GROUND DARK-ROAST COFFEE BEANS

4 CUPS (32 OUNCES) WATER

MILK OF YOUR CHOICE *(optional)*

SUGAR OR SWEETENER *(optional)*

Using a drip coffee maker, place the coffee grounds in a coffee filter,

add the water to the chamber and push the button. Ah, the simplicity of

the good old days! Pour the brewed coffee into the cup of your choice.

Add milk and sugar if desired.

Makes up to 3 servings depending on cup size

Black Tea Ideas

"There's a great deal of poetry and fine sentiment in a chest of tea."
—Ralph Waldo Emerson

Some truly inspired ideas require tea—the blacker the better. These can be your rainy day, snuggled-up-with-a-good-book ideas, or they can be your not-feeling-well, need-to-be-in-bed ideas. Either requires a soothing cup of tea and some blank pages. Note your Black Tea Ideas here.

Black Tea

1 BAG BLACK TEA OR 1 OUNCE LOOSE-LEAF ENGLISH BREAKFAST, EARL GREY, DARJEELING, OR ASSAM TEA

2 CUPS (16 OUNCES) WATER

MILK OF YOUR CHOICE *(optional)*

SUGAR, HONEY, OR SWEETENER *(optional)*

Place the tea bag, or loose-leaf tea in an infuser, into a tea cup or mug.

Bring the water to a boil and then pour into the cup, allowing 4 to 5 minutes

to steep. Add milk and sugar if desired.

Makes 1 serving

CHAI IDEAS

"A cup of tea says to the brain, Now, rise, and show your strength. Be eloquent, and deep, and tender; see, with a clear eye, into nature and into life; spread your white wings of quivering thought, and soar..." —Jerome K. Jerome, *Three Men in a Boat (To Say Nothing of the Dog!)*

Some ideas require many ingredients to blend in order to create a delicious outcome. In addition to caffeinated inspiration, they require complex flavors that work together to make the whole more than the sum of its parts. The ideas and dreams that need synergy to come to fruition are your Chai Ideas. Thoughts must be gathered and considered, ground down to their essence. While these ideas may be more work to fulfill, the rich, spicy outcome is worth the toil and time.

Chai

3 CARDAMOM PODS, *gently crushed*

2 WHOLE BLACK PEPPERCORNS OR 1 PINCH BLACK PEPPER

2 WHOLE CLOVES OR 1 PINCH GROUND CLOVES

⅛ TEASPOON GROUND GINGER

1 CINNAMON STICK OR ½ TEASPOON GROUND CINNAMON

1 TEASPOON BROWN SUGAR

1 PINCH GROUND STAR ANISE

½ TEASPOON VANILLA

1 PINCH NUTMEG

1 CUP (8 OUNCES) WATER

1 BAG BLACK TEA OR 1 OUNCE LOOSE-LEAF BLACK TEA

1 CUP (8 OUNCES) MILK OF YOUR CHOICE

Place all ingredients except the tea and milk in a saucepan and bring to a boil. Reduce the heat to low, cover, and simmer for 15 minutes before removing from heat. Add the tea bag, or loose tea in an infuser, and let steep for 5 minutes. Pour mixture through a strainer into a large mug or tall coffee glass. Add milk and sugar if desired.

Makes 1 serving

COFFEEHOUSE IDEAS

"The powers of a man's mind are directly proportionate to the quantity of coffee he drinks." —James Mackintosh

At times, it is impossible to go it alone. To work out an incomplete idea or gain inspiration, you need to reach outside of yourself. You need more than your own caffeinated thoughts; you need to bounce ideas off a friend or a fellow drinker. These are your Coffeehouse Ideas. Jot down your half-baked musings here and then go get some outside help!

Coffeehouse

Walk, drive, or ride to your neighborhood coffeehouse.

Buy your favorite caffeinated concoction and enjoy! Ahh!

Sometimes you just can't do it on your own.

Zucchero

A WHO'S WHO OF THE CAFFEINATED AND INSPIRED:

Gary Larson, *contemporary cartoonist*

Gustave Flaubert, *19th century French novelist*

Honoré de Balzac, *19th century French novelist and playwright*

James Mackintosh, *18th to 19th century Scottish philosopher, journalist, and politician*

Jerome K. Jerome, *19th to 20th century British novelist, actor and playwright*

Johanne Sebastian Bach, *17th to 18th century German composer*

Phil Ford, *British contemporary author*

Ralph Waldo Emerson, *19th century essayist and poet*

Roman Payne, *contemporary novelist*

T. S. Eliot, *19th to 20th century poet*